About the Author

I am a retired Surgeon and have lived in the north-east of Scotland for many years. I am the author of numerous medical articles, with an occasional venture into golfing subjects. I have always been keen on active sport. Cricket was my main sport in my teens and early twenties. However, the approaching thirties saw me turn to golf. I became an occasional three, but a steady four handicap was the best I could achieve. Strangely enough, I believe it is this combination of medical knowledge, along with being a "nearly" good golfer that has given me the insight into what constitutes the main "bridge" that the poorer golfer must cross in order to achieve any quantum leap forward in golfing skills. The leap may only be a percentage. In other words, fifty per cent for a four handicap will only get a player down to a two handicap. But for a twenty handicap golfer, the potential target is ten handicap. That is a massive improvement.

In my early years, I had a close and happy family life. 'Work hard and play hard' seems to sum up my teens and twenties. A marriage to Patricia, and a family of two sons has added the icing to the cake. A consultant appointment in Aberdeen, and a research project in later years proved extremely fulfilling. The thoughts contained in this book have been swirling around in my mind for many years, but retirement has given me the time to crystallise my thoughts, and this short book is the result. If it achieves a minor breakthrough in the teaching and understanding of the golf swing, I will indeed be a happy man.

Kerr About Golf

Come Swing Along with Me

Neill Watson Kerr

Kerr About Golf
Come Swing Along with Me

Olympia Publishers

London

www.olympiapublishers.com

OLYMPIA PAPERBACK EDITION

A CIP catalogue record for this title is
available from the British Library.

ISBN: 978-1-78830-220-3

First Published in 2019

Olympia Publishers
60 Cannon Street
London
EC4N 6NP

Printed in Great Britain

Dedication

To my wife, Patricia, and my two sons, Angus and
Duncan. The game of golf has been one of the many
threads that has given us so many happy family times
together.

Acknowledgments

A big thank you to my younger son, Duncan, for posing for the golf swing photographs. Also, to Angus, for his immense help with the computer aspect of things. To hear the heavenly words, "That's OK, Dad, you can send it now." Music in one's ears!

Contents

Foreword

I am delighted that my fellow Aberdonian, Harry Bannerman has agreed to write a short foreword to my book. Harry is a legend amongst golfers. A member of the Ryder Cup team of 1971, he played at the Old Warson Country Club, St Louis, Missouri. This was in an era when Great Britain stood alone against the invincible golfing might of the Americans, and a time when Arnold Palmer and Jack Nicklaus were at their peak. For Harry to gain two and a half points from an away match was an outstanding achievement. Harry was the "Jiménez" of his time, enjoyed a monster cigar after the game, and was always ready with a quip and a cheery smile. The American press took to their "Cigar-smoking Bannerman". Sadly, Harry's back continued to plague him over the next few years and he was eventually forced to give up tournament golf. Totally undaunted, Harry took up teaching with a consuming interest, and spent some sixteen years teaching in Germany before returning to his native Aberdeenshire to continue his teaching career.

Harry has given me a brief summary of some of the playing highlights of his career.

Member of the PGA for over fifty-two years; former Ryder Cup player (played five matches, winning two, losing two & halving one; the halved match was against none other than Arnold Palmer). US Masters contestant 1972, tied thirty-third. He received his invitation from the President of Augusta National Golf Club, the legendary Bobby Jones (many cherished memories of that event). Eight appearances in the Open Championship; five times to the last day. Best finish: tied eleventh. Out in thirty at Royal Muirfield in the fourth round in 1972, tied nineteenth. Twice Scottish Professional Golf Champion: 1967 at Montrose and 1972 at Strathaven. The winning margin on the latter occasion was ten strokes.

"Neill is a passionate golfer, and, with his vast medical knowledge, is confident that he is able to give hope, and help the average golfer in his quest for improvement. I am sure his book will act as a useful precursor to those unsure of what to expect from professional golf tuition. It takes the form of a pre-tuition eye-opener.

For me, golf is a test of character and an attitude of the mind, and some of my favourite golfing clichés are: The hands are the only contact we have with the club. All the great players I have played with all had a repetitive rhythmic pre-shot routine. The hands are the transmission of the centrifugal force. The club head hits the ball. Conclusion – it is important how we place our hands on the club. Grip pressure: firm for big shots, and light for short shots. Glove on for the drives but off for putts.

Neill's book is a fascinating insight into some of the problems facing the higher handicap golfers, and there is no doubting that basic swing problems do exist. The text is about the nuts and bolts of the swing, rather than the finished article. It is an interesting read, and I do hope that my small contribution by way of this foreword will be useful to your enjoyment of Neill's book."

The Will-O'-the-Wisp Golf Swing

Why is it that a powerful, consistent and conventional golf swing is so difficult for most of us to perform? We tend to reach a threshold level of execution and understanding of the swing movement reasonably quickly, but, from that point on, any further improvement is either painfully slow, or non-existent. Any handicap reductions we may make are more likely to be the result of improvements in the short game, or better course management, rather than an improvement of the swing itself. On the odd occasion when we may discover a reasonably functional version of the golf swing, inevitably someone will criticise it, stating that this or that is wrong, and will then attempt to correct your stance, grip or whatever. Nothing seems to allow us to mimic the pattern of the professional swings that we see on the television screen, week in and week out.

Why this should be so, is an extremely difficult question to answer. However, in these few chapters I hope to enlighten you as to the reasons why the golf swing is so difficult for most of us to perform. On the other hand, it can be an apparently simple and straightforward action for so many others. Once we can understand and appreciate just what the stumbling blocks are, it will then become a much easier task to explain and understand the various pathways each of us may follow if we wish to improve our game and achieve a more functional, repetitive, and enjoyable golf swing.

It is well known that tension and stress play a major part in breaking down a smooth and functional swing. How else could Doug Saunders have missed that tiddler of a putt on the eighteenth green at St Andrews to lose the Open Championship to Jack Nicklaus – a putt he would have sunk ninety-nine times out of a hundred? How else could Jordan Spieth have produced the awful strokes he did on the twelfth hole in the final round of the Masters Tournament in 2016? Again, how else could Jean Van de Velde in 1999 have literally thrown the Open Championship away at the last hole? But, having said this, such severe stress of this nature is not part and parcel of our club's monthly medal or knockout competitions, so I think we can eliminate stress as a material factor in the inconsistency of our handicap swings.

Rational thought on the subject of the golf swing would suggest that it ought to be a reasonably simple movement for us to perform; our ball stays still, our equipment is precision-designed, the ground is level for a drive, and the ball is even perched on a little peg. Nevertheless, despite all these considerable advantages, it remains an inescapable fact that most medium to high-handicap golfers hit far more poor shots than they ever strike either long, straight or accurate.

Many have sought answers as to why the vast majority of us are such poor strikers of the ball. Indeed, a never-ending succession of professional tournament players, who have amassed vast fortunes on the golfing circuits of the world, have attempted to pass on to us their knowledge, either by visual means or by that of the written word. Their advice is sound, and often inventively put over. Nevertheless, despite such priceless revelations, the realisation of the dream for most of us remains little more than a tantalising expectation.

The foundation stones of professional tuition tend to be based on certain concepts. First and foremost is the acquisition of a good sound grip and set-up position. After this will come an explanation of the actual swing movements, along with advice as to the important positional or mechanical gates one must pass through at each stage of the swing. Following this will come the practical attempts to put all the information into an integrated, balanced and smooth golf swing. Finally, the pupil will be encouraged to practise diligently, and not attempt to try for power until later.

Sensible enough reasoning. A good grip, a sound set-up position, an understanding of the swing mechanics, and then intensive practice: these really ought to be the corner-stones of success. However, as we all know only too well, rarely does this hold true in practice. Many of us work extremely hard on our swings, we do seek tuition, we do understand what we have been told, and we do practise diligently. More often than not, it is of little avail. For a short time, on the practice ground or on the course, we may feel that we are on the verge of discovering the ingredients of a sound, repetitive and grooved swing: the swing that will put us on the fairways off the tee, the swing that will give us precision and accuracy with the irons, and the swing that will remain repeatable hole after hole and day after day. Indeed, most of us have felt at some time or another that we were almost on the threshold of achieving such a goal, only to find that the elation and euphoria of our 'eureka' moment inevitably plunges into the disaster and despair of the next.

Such is the pattern of golf for most of us. We flit from one modification to another, always tinkering, always searching. Occasionally we are partly successful, and a reasonably steady and stable swing will appear for a time. We appreciate that it is not precisely what we are looking for, but at least it affords us a measure of consistency, and gets us round the course without too many disasters. However, once we try and build on this, as likely as not, precisely the opposite effect happens, and we are cast back in no man's land again. The odd thing is that on the rare occasions when we do achieve a really perfect shot, it seems to come right out of the blue; it just seems to happen, a perfect combination of every part of the body with no strain or effort, just one cohesive functioning movement of the body and club. If we can do it once, why can't we do it again?

Golf literature provides us with very few explanations as to this will-o'-the-wisp golf swing phenomenon. Indeed, one might almost suggest that explanations are tactfully avoided, as it is not good business to put forward the view that the golf swing is not reproducible in everybody. Many golf professionals do take an extremely positive line on this, and stoutly maintain that a good golf swing is reproducible in everyone, provided the pupil will follow their instructions and practice diligently. I would certainly agree that a reasonably functional golf swing is achievable by all fit and healthy individuals, but I would question whether a swing that is both classic *and powerful* is completely within the grasp of each and every one of us.

Analysis of the better players shows that the possession of a sound swing does not appear to be related to the amount of tuition, nor to physical build or any quantifiable assessment of intelligence. I do not say that practice, tuition, physique and intelligence are not of use, of course they are. However, there is not as direct a relationship between these assets and the acquisition of a good sound golf swing as many might have us believe. Top-class golfers come in all shapes and sizes, and competent powerful swingers of the club tend to show their prowess right from the first time they take up the game. We all know of golfers who have practised little, have had virtually no tuition and yet play to low single figure handicaps with almost monotonous regularity. Nick Faldo only took up the game at the late age of fourteen, yet was winning top amateur awards three or four years later and Ryder Cup honours by the age of twenty. Seve Ballesteros was an established world star by the same age. Rory McIlroy has taken the golfing world by storm in his teens, and Jordan Spieth is a class golfer, setting the golfing world alight in his early twenties. There simply has to be a lot more to golfing prowess than can be explained by an infatuation with the game, good tuition or intensive practise.

Let's delve a little deeper into this intriguing question of who may possesses, or fail to possess, "natural golfing ability". Indeed, just what is "natural golfing ability"? Why do some individuals seem to have the inborn skill to swing the club well almost from the first time they hold it? Is there an ingredient that is common to all good golfers, but which is missing from their handicap brethren? If there is, and if we can discover what this missing link is, maybe we can induce it or compensate for it in some way.

Such questions have rightly concerned golfers and scientists over the years, and much thought and research has been undertaken. It would be invidious to mention any particular golf book and claim that it was superior to others; all undoubtedly have their merits. However, Ben Hogan's contribution, *The Modern Fundamentals of Golf*, published way back in 1957, was a landmark in golf tuition. His book was then, and still remains, a masterpiece of description. In his book, Hogan described and illustrated the swing with absolute clarity and meticulous attention to detail. He described and analysed all possible aspects of the swing: the grip, the stance, the backswing, the downswing, the plane of the swing, in fact just about every position of every muscle and joint in the body. Each and every facet came under his expert scrutiny. His book has remained a classic text on anatomical positional golf tuition, and, in it, Hogan undoubtedly set a standard for many others to follow. Yet, despite Hogan's praiseworthy and meticulous attention to detail, it failed to give us the full story. A vital ingredient was missing, and it is this same ingredient that is missing from nearly every other instructional book or piece of advice written about the golf swing. Hogan himself appreciated this, but, unfortunately, he died without revealing the ultimate secret of the golf swing. I wonder whether we can now discover what this secret might be?

Almost all instructional books (could it be because the written word is not the ideal medium through which to teach movements?) tend to fail in their attempts to communicate to the reader the complete story of *how* to swing the golf club and strike the ball. They certainly tell us what the correct mechanical movements are supposed to be; however, they fail to tell us how to convert this mass of anatomical and mechanical information into a vital, live and active swing movement. Most persist with the conviction that accurate positional and anatomical detail simply must be the pathway to a perfect swing. I certainly agree that this is a large part of the answer; however, it is only one part, and the practical evidence of generations of tuition and teaching, good though much of it is, has failed to produce the results for the vast majority of club golfers. There still remains a missing factor, and it is this factor that the average golfer simply must know more about if he or she is to improve above a certain initial level of skill.

In recent years, scientists have tried to improve on this rather limited approach to golf tuition. They have investigated the physics of the swing, in the belief that an explanation of the actual mechanics of the golf swing will provide the pupil with a better mental image of the type of movement he or she is required to produce. In so doing, these scientific researchers have certainly taken golf tuition one further step along the road. However, to encapsulate their findings into a mathematical formula is hardly likely to be of much help to the average golfer. Nevertheless, these theorists have produced fascinating information concerning the action of the arms, the wrists and the club shaft, which have the nature of a simple mechanical flail system. Such writers have emphasised the necessity of turning the shoulders, the requirement to cock the wrists, and the importance of releasing the clubhead at the ball in a flail action. However, as regards actually undertaking the actual live swing movement they still leave the prospective golfer with little in the way of a completely satisfying answer. Their contribution may well be a much more sophisticated explanation of what is supposed to happen during the swing, but it still falls some way short of the required explanation of how to make it happen, or how to make all the data relevant to each and every one of us with our own individual and unique body proportions and instinctive movements.

Many professional teachers are aware of this deficiency, and attempt to overcome the problem by stressing and emphasising particular component parts of the swing. They may use descriptive phrases such as "lead with your left side" or "throw your bottom at the ball" or "feel as if you are balancing a tray with your right hand at the top of the back swing". These phrases and many more like them, using the word "feel", are attempts by the instructor to impart to the pupil the sensations they themselves have, and which they consider that the pupil ought to be able to achieve. It is certainly a serious attempt to supply the factor that will link the individual movements into an integrated and total whole. However, the problem is that they are essentially subjective phrases that are made up from the teacher's or player's own personal experience, and, as such, may not be applicable with any degree of reliability or consistency to other individuals. Being a subjective-style approach, this approach will only be totally meaningful if the pupil is of the same bodily make-up and balance as the instructor.

Video techniques have proved to be helpful, and the Faldo/Leadbetter tapes were amongst the first to demonstrate training techniques such as tucking a towel under the armpits, or keeping the club shaft into the belly button. They are undoubtedly useful additions to the spoken word. However, they still lack a common thread which might link them to any or all handicap golfers with swing problems.

I heard recently that the technical experts have invented a machine which, once you insert the appropriate software, guides you through the swing path of any famous golfer whose action you might wish to copy. A rather expensive toy, I would suggest, but perhaps more useful for those with an already grooved swing. I fear that such gimmicks are of little use to the average handicap golfer.

I remember the first occasion on which I came face to face with the apparent deficiency of professional tuition. I was a raw young student of eighteen years of age, and, at the time, was playing reasonably well to a seven handicap. My swing was functional and repetitive, but rather ungainly, and I tended to strike the ball with the weight falling towards the back foot. I decided I had little chance of improving without expert help, and arranged a series of lessons with the club professional. I went to these lessons buoyed up with enthusiasm and hope. I was prepared to work hard. I expected to be given the secret and insight into the perfect swing. To my bitter disappointment, the advice I received was that my swing, grip and set-up was reasonable and I should alter very little. The professional suggested I concentrate all my efforts on trying to get my weight through at impact. "How"? I asked. "Oh, you just have to do it" he replied. That was it! (I may add that this would not have happened today, as our club professionals are now highly trained, and have all passed fairly stiff examinations before being qualified as golf tutors.)

I remember coming away from this lesson a very dispirited and disappointed young man. The professional had in the end told me little that my friends had not already advised. I knew I hit the ball off the back foot; what I wanted from him was advice on how to get the weight over, not just to be told to get it over. I had been trying to do that myself throughout the previous year with little success. I remember having, at the time, convinced myself, with all the naivety of youth, that golf professionals as a group were undoubtedly in a dastardly plot together, and had connived amongst themselves to hide the ultimate secret of the golf swing and prevent the amateur from getting in on it. This was back in the days before the great surge in golf interest. A stupid thought, I know, and, with more maturity, I realised what an absurd idea it was. The simple fact was that the particular club professional whom I had used was a creditable performer on the course, but not of the highest calibre as a teacher of the game. Nevertheless, despite the disappointments of this experience, I still retained a sneaking feeling at the back of my mind that somewhere in my immature thoughts there had to be a few grains of truth. That feeling continued to haunt me over the years, but, whenever I tried to rationalise it further, I still could not find complete answers. Why are certain individuals almost instinctively able to play better golf than others? In fact, are the professionals actually holding back on something?

It has been said that "Man will occasionally stumble over the truth, but most of the time he will pick himself up and continue on". It took me many years before I realised I had in fact stumbled over a truth of sorts in these far off days.

I have now discovered the secret that that professional denied to me all those years ago, the secret that he and most other professionals and top amateurs possess, but find it incredibly difficult to pass it on with any success. Indeed, what I discovered has to be the same long-lost secret that Ben Hogan failed to pass on to future golfing generations. Since discovering this common thread to all golf swings, I can now add the "how" to the "do" of the golf swing. Let's see if I can impart this knowledge to you over the course of the next few chapters.

I regard the information in this book as fitting into the situation in which a regular player, who has achieved a fairly standard swing and a medium to high handicap, then wishes to improve his or her game, and thinks about arranging for expert tuition. I mean no disrespect to our expert tutors, and I am sure they will actually agree with this statement, when I say that, in most situations, there is only so much that can be achieved, and it is only very rarely that a "silk purse can be made out of a sow's ear." It is at this precise point that I feel the contents of this small volume will come in as extremely useful. I am certainly not claiming that I will be the one to realise the alchemist's dream, but I feel that the information contained herein will go a long way along this path, and, if this book is read before tuition, it will make every pupil/teacher experience a much more profitable and rewarding experience for both parties.

The Bare Bones of the Classic Golf Swing

If we are to understand both the mechanics of the golf swing and the motivating forces responsible for such movements, then a useful starting point is to look at just how our framework (which is made up of our bones and joints) goes about its task of performing the classic golf swing movements. Following on from this we can look at just how our muscular system goes about its task of bringing about these required movements. It sounds complicated, but it isn't really, and descriptions along these lines begins to make a lot more sense of the average club golfer's perennial problem of a massive and permanent inconsistency between intent and execution.

At this point in the script, I would suggest that the reader moves fairly rapidly through both this chapter and the next. Don't get bogged down in detail, just get the gist of the contents and the basic actions required, and move rapidly on.

As far as golfing movements are concerned we can divide our skeleton into two separate and distinct mechanical units.

The first of these units is made up of the spine, pelvis and the legs (coloured red in Fig. 1). The second skeletal unit is made up of the shoulder-blades, collarbones, arms and hands, along with the addition of the golf club itself (coloured black in Fig. 1). Each of these skeletal units (plus club, in the second instance) is a distinct and separate mechanical entity. They have their own identity, and their own particular roles to play in the golf swing. However, the end result has to be that these two separate units combine and work together in harmony as one sequenced swing movement.

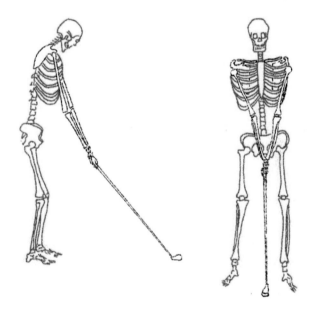

Figure. 1 The head, chest, spine and legs skeletal complex (red). The shoulder-blades, collarbones, arms and club complex (black).

Let's look at each group of bones separately, and then at the linking mechanism which allows them to function together as if they were one integrated unit.

THE SPINE, PELVIS AND LEGS MECHANICAL COMPLEX – THE VERTICAL UNIT

In this complex, the bones include the skull, the bones of the spine, the chest or rib-cage, the oval shaped pelvic bone, and the two legs: in fact, the whole of the skeleton except for the two shoulder-blades, the two collarbones and the two arms (Fig. 2). This complex of bones has only two mechanical functions to perform. The first is vertical support. The second is rotation, or twisting around a central spinal axis.

__The Supportive Action__ - In this, the legs, pelvis, spine and chest (coloured in red in Fig. 1) act as a vertical support column, with the main aim being to provide three stable suspension points, from which the second unit, the two shoulder-blades, the two arms and the club will suspend and act (from now on I will refer to this second unit as "The Flail Unit"). The three suspension points are the mid-line neck spine, and both sides of the upper back of the chest (Fig. 2). The Flail Unit will not be able to function effectively and repetitively unless the neck spine of the vertical unit remains at a fixed point in space throughout the whole swing movement. During the swing, the neck spine may, and will, twist and turn quite freely. However, neither it nor the skull should move to any great extent, either laterally or vertically, throughout the swing action. It is this neck, spine, and upper chest stability that provides the Flail Unit with the firm suspension points from which it can suspend and

28

carry out its allotted task. The repetitive nature of the golf swing relies entirely upon the upper spine support's being constant in both the vertical and lateral direction throughout the whole swing. One remembers reading how Jack Grout used to grasp young Jack Nicklaus's hair while he swung the club. This was Grout's method of ensuring that his pupil's upper spinal vertical and lateral stability was maintained throughout the body's rotatory action. The spine is obviously aided in its vertical support action if the spinal column is kept fairly straight i.e. the straight back.

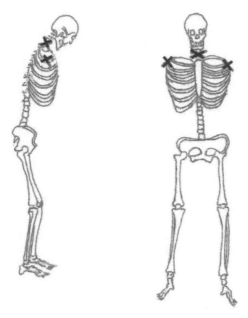

Figure. 2 Head, chest, spine and legs skeletal unit seen as a separate unit – also showing the three suspension points of the flail system.

The Spinal Twisting or Rotary Action – This is the second required action of the vertical skeletal unit. It requires that the spine, chest, trunk and upper legs be rotated or twisted round in a corkscrew fashion from the neck to the knees during the backswing. The lower legs, from the knees down to the ground, *do not take an active part in this rotation.* Their task is to resist the upper leg, body and chest rotation occurring above them by acting as dual buffers to that rotary movement. In other words, the legs below the knee must act as two firm, but flexible pillars of stability and support that are solidly anchored to the ground throughout the backswing (Fig. 3). They must do this because it is the lower legs that must initiate the downswing movement and the return rotation of the upper body and chest. In order to do this, it is essential that the both feet remain in firm contact with the ground, so that they may act as the springboard for the return downswing action. Any excessive left knee or ankle flexing during the backswing will break this essential firm platform for the initiation of the downswing action. Furthermore, the vertical supportive action will also be compromised, and the head is more likely to move vertically and laterally, destroying the repetitive nature of the swing. Remember: neck-to-knees rotation, and, below that, knees-to-ground stability and preparation for the return action.

Figure 3 shows the two planes that mark the upper and lower boundaries of the body and the spine's muscular tube-like rotatory movement. One can regard the relatively stable knees as being the actual base of the backswing rotatory movement.

The downswing movement is triggered from the feet to knee area, and results in a spinal and body de-rotation movement which works up the spine and spins the upper chest back round towards the set-up position. By doing this, it must, of necessity, carry round with it the two shoulder-blades and arms. It is this movement that triggers the two-rod flail action from the shoulder-blades, which culminates in the second rod of the flail, i.e. the club shaft, whipping or flailing the clubhead into and through the ball.

The skeletal action of the downswing results in the vertical skeletal unit assuming a very rigid left side from the left heel to the upper left shoulder – the so called "braced left side." It is against this firm left side that the two-rod flail unit (i.e. arms plus club shaft) can pour a lot of right arm power into the final flailing action of the clubhead into the ball.

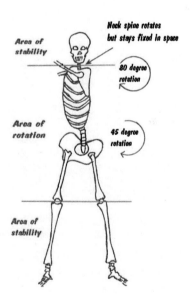

Figure. 3 Twisting or rotational movement of the chest, spine and upper leg skeletal complex

From the impact position, the upper body will continue to rotate round, with the right heel lifting and the whole body complex continuing into the follow-through position.

Throughout all the trunk and leg rotatory movement, the neck spine must remain in the same place in space – rotated and turned, yes, but not moved very much, either vertically or laterally.

In summary – the mechanical requirements of the vertical spine and leg skeletal unit on the backswing (Fig. 1 red) are, firstly, to provide a firm upper neck and back of the chest

Figure. 4 Four photographs of golfers and their 'below knee positions' at the top of their swings. All have their feet firmly on the ground. Number four has his left knee turned in slightly but his initial move of the downswing is a quick and firm shift of the left knee and lower leg forward. Below knee stability allows powerful muscle stretching above.

stability for the base of the Flail Unit (coloured black Fig. 1); and, secondly, to undertake neck-to-knee spinal rotation. The lower legs from the two knees down must act as two pillars of resistance, with their action being to buffer and brace against the rotary movement occurring above them. Following this action, their now stretched muscles will initiate the return downswing action.

Figure 4 shows four professional golfers at their top of the swing positions. The first three are quite obviously poised to initiate the downswing movement with their knees and below, but the fourth has his left knee turned in slightly. However, his feet are still flat on the ground, and his first movement is a rapid straightening of the left knee and bracing of the whole left skeletal structure which initiates the de-rotation of the pelvis and spine.

I remember once watching a well-known English professional at the Open at Royal Birkdale. I had the distinct impression that he could have been playing in divers' lead boots, so glued to the ground were the soles of his feet.

THE SECOND SKELETAL UNIT - THE SHOULDERS, ARMS AND CLUB SKELETAL COMPLEX – THE FLAIL UNIT.

This skeletal unit is a completely separate and distinct entity from that of the legs and spine, and has an entirely different function. This complex of bones and joints also includes the golf club (coloured black in Fig. 1, and seen as a separate and isolated unit in Fig. 5). The mechanical action required from this combination of shoulder-blades, collarbones, arms, hands and golf club is known as the "The two-rod Flail

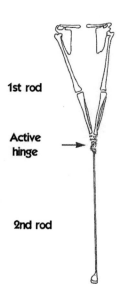

1st rod

Active hinge →

2nd rod

Figure. 5 Two-rod flail unit

Action". The principle of this is quite simple, and may be considered as a mechanical device made up of two rods, linked together by a flexible hinge. Such a flail system (Fig. 6) was used by the Ancient Egyptians for threshing corn (and in the UK even up to the early twentieth century). The first rod (A) is held in the hands and swept down towards the corn. The second rod, which is hinged loosely to it by a leather thong, follows at much the same pace, initially; hence the angle between the two rods remains much the same at first (Fig. 6, B and C). Now, if both rods are to reach the horizontal position at the same time, it is necessary for the periphery of the second rod, somewhere along the arc, to start travelling very much faster than the first rod. It is

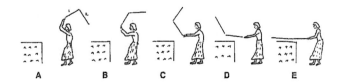

A   B   C   D   E

Figure.6 The principle of the flail system

possible to hold this acceleration back towards the end of

34

the movement, with the result that the periphery of the second rod is whipped through the final few degrees of the movement with an ever-increasing speed. This is achieved by virtually "throwing away" the second rod and gaining speed by generating centrifugal force from the base (Fig. 6, C, D, E). If any of us were given a simple two-rod flail system to experiment with, we would find little difficulty in achieving a reasonable flail action. We would find that we were capable of whipping the second rod in at the last second; and the more whip or flail we could achieve towards the end of the movement, the greater would be the speed at the periphery of the second rod. If, however, we were inefficient in our whipping action, and let the angle between the two rods open up towards a straight line at the start of the movement, then we would have destroyed or "used up" the centrifugal force, by generating it too early in the sequence, and might accomplish the task rather better with a single straight rod. The point where the two rods come into alignment ought to be the point of maximum speed for the clubhead, and this is therefore the ideal impact area between the flail and the corn – or, in the golf swing, the club-head and the ball. The other point to notice is that the control of this simple two rod flail system is at the base of the first rod.

The base of our first rod is made up of four bones, our two flat triangular shaped shoulder-blades situated at the upper back of the chest, and our two collarbones at the upper front of the chest (Fig. 7). These form a group of four bones, making up an almost complete bone ring, external to the upper chest and encircling it from the front to the back. However, this ring is not fully complete: the back of the ring is open, and there are no bone or joint connections between the two inner aspects of our shoulder-blades and the mid-line spine at the back of the chest. These two points are merely linked by muscles (green in Fig. 10) and this gives our two shoulder-blades considerable freedom of

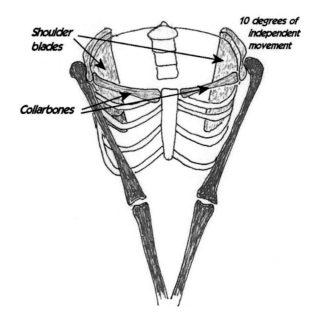

Figure. 7 The base of the flail unit (speckled green) encircles the chest, the two arms (red) extend from the periphery of the shoulder-blades.

independent movement around the upper back of the chest. Not so for the front of the ring; our two collarbones are much more restricted in their lateral movement, as their inner ends are attached to the mid-line of the chest at the front and the other end to the outer aspect of the shoulder-blades. So, the base of our first rod is this three-quarter ring of bone, semi-fixed at the front and side, but much more flexible and moveable at the back.

Our two arms extend downwards from sockets set in the periphery of our two flat plate-like shoulder-blades. With our two hands united at the grip this makes up a triangular frame of bone. Let's call this bone triangle the first rod of our two-rod Flail System. The second rod is the golf club, which is gripped by the two hands, and our wrists constitute the hinge between the two rods. The crucial point of all this somewhat long-winded anatomical description is that the triangular first rod and the golf club must combine to form *one* mechanically functional two rod flail system, with its sole purpose being to allow the head of the club (the end of the second rod) to hit (or flail into) the ball at the maximum speed possible, consistent with being accurate and having the ability to be repetitive.

It ought to be reasonably simple to achieve this. However, in our case, there are some complications. Unfortunately for us, the first rod of our flail system is not a simple single rod system. As we have seen our first rod is a bone triangle, of which the base is a three-quarter bone ring around the upper chest. The length of the first rod is reasonably straightforward, as it is our two arms extending down to the grip; but here again, our grip must not only act as the link between our two arms; it must also act as both a flexible, and at one and the same time, active hinge between the two rods. It must form the swing plane and the flail angle between the two rods on the backswing, and then, when the final flail or whip in at the ball occurs, it must help to direct the clubface, and add muscular power to any centrifugal force that has been generated from the shoulders.

As one can imagine, this degree of complexity makes for a somewhat fragile and easily disrupted first rod mechanism. However, for a good repetitive golf swing action to take place this bone triangle *must act throughout the swing as if it were one single and simple rod.* There are big problems ahead!

In the next chapter, we will see just how the link between the vertical skeletal unit and the base of the flail unit must function if the integrity of the triangular first rod is to be maintained throughout the swing sequence.

First Rod of the Flail – The Multi-Boned Triangle that Must Act as One Single Rod

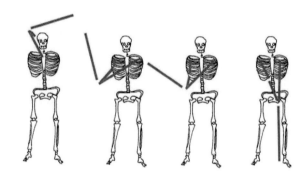

Figure. 8 Concept of the flail action required in the golf swing

In the previous chapter, we learnt about the two separate skeletal units of the human skeleton, and how they have their own individual actions, yet must combine their actions to produce one functioning golf swing. Figure 1 illustrates the two separate skeletal units, while Figure 8 illustrates the sort of flail action we require from the two-rod mechanical unit.

Ensuring the correct mechanical action between the upper chest and the base of the flail unit is paramount; if we get it wrong, there is no way back for that swing. Only the correct functioning of this connection will ensure a smooth transfer movement between the two skeletal units.

In the last chapter I mentioned not to ponder over detail, but to read right through the chapter and get the broad concepts of what is required of our skeleton in terms of mechanical movements. I suggest the same here: don't dwell, move on.

First, let's look at the triangular shaped first rod of the two-rod flail unit, and see how it manages to functions as if it were one single rod. We have the base of the triangle, which is the two-shoulder-blade/collarbone ring. We have the length of the rod, which is made up of the two arms; and we have the apex of the triangle which is the grip. Let's look in more detail at this triangle of bones, and see how they are able to function as one single first rod. To do this necessitates three constants being present in the triangle throughout the swing.

The Three Necessary Constants of the Triangular Shaped First Rod

(1) The Base. It is crucial that the width of the base (i.e. the distance between the outer aspects of the two shoulder-blades) remains as a constant throughout the swing.

(2) The arm length from the base to the apex or grip must also remain a constant.

(3) The grip or hinge at the apex of the triangle must remain firm but flexibly united throughout the whole swing.

If any one of these constants fails to function correctly, it will become impossible for the first rod to maintain its integrity as a single rod, and, as a result, the whole swing process will be disrupted. These three requirements are so interrelated that to disrupt one will automatically destroy the others, and the first rod will fail to function as intended. In other words, no classic swing will be possible. Let's take each one in turn.

1) Maintenance of the width of the base of the triangle
A constant width of the base of the triangle during its

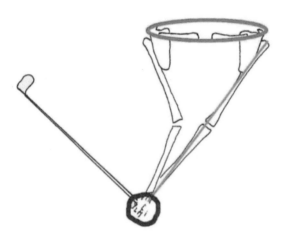

Figure. 9 Three constants of the 1st rod of the flail system

rotation on the backswing and downswing is an absolute must. This base, as we have learnt, is the three-quarter oval osseous ring around the upper chest, and is made up of the two shoulder-blades at the back and the two collarbones at the front. These four bones are all external to the chest wall (Fig. 9 the green ring, and Fig. 10 the speckled green ring).

Figure. 10 The base of the flail unit (speckled green) encircling the chest. The two arms (red) extending from the periphery. The remainder of the circle (green) is muscle attached from the shoulder-blades to the spine

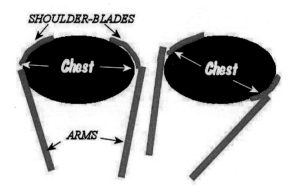

Figure. 11 Diagrammatic cross-section view of the full amount of independent turning of the two shoulder-blades acting together

It is not always easy to get the two shoulder-blades to turn in unison and take-up their thirty to forty degrees of independent freedom of movement relative to the chest. However, it must be done. Figure 11 shows in a diagrammatic fashion the initial independent turning movement of the two shoulder blades.

From this point on, the only way that the shoulder-blades and arms can turn any further round is for the whole upper chest to turn round and carry the two shoulder-blades

Figure. 12 The one-piece takeaway. Basically shoulder-blade action alone

round with it in piggy-back fashion. The initial tightening movement of the two shoulder-blades has been termed "the one-piece takeaway" and it is seen diagrammatically in Figure 11, and being carried out by a golfer in Figure 12. From this point on, the whole upper chest must then rotate round and carry the constant width base of the flail unit round with it. We have now completed the full backswing movement of the base of the flail unit (Figs. 13 and 14).

Figure. 13 Full upper chest plus shoulder-blades rotation

Failure to complete the one-piece takeaway correctly is the most common cause of a handicap golfer's swing breaking down. The reason why they fail is because the amount of freedom of movement of each individual shoulder-blade makes it all too easy to allow one shoulder-blade to turn further than the other. If this happens — and it most certainly will if there is any tendency for a side dominant muscular action to take control (as there is for the majority of us, as most of us are right side dominant in our muscular actions) — then any classic swing is lost from that point on. With the base of the first rod disrupted, along with it will go the integrity of the whole first rod.

Interestingly enough, due to the anatomical make-up of the two shoulder-blade base, if the base is pushed round by controlled muscular movement from the left shoulder, and the left shoulder is turned round and under the chin, this will have an entirely beneficial effect on maintenance of the width of the base.

Figure. 14 Full turn of the base of the flail unit

In fact, just what we want. The left side action achieves this, because, if the four-bone ring is pushed from the left, it tends to push all four bones round as a single intact unit, whereas attempting to pull the base round by retracting the right shoulder-blade does precisely the opposite, and actually pulls the base apart.

Try this yourself now: stand square, arms drooping down, pull your right shoulder-blade up and back. It is very

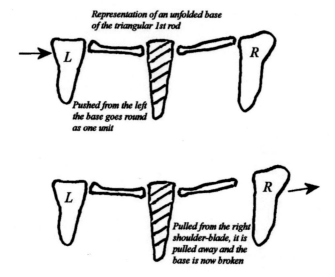

Representation of an unfolded base of the triangular 1st rod

Pushed from the left the base goes round as one unit

Pulled from the right shoulder-blade, it is pulled away and the base is now broken

Figure. 15 Effect on the base of the 1st rod triangle by being pushed from the left or pulled from the right

easy to do this, and no movement is required of the left shoulder. Now try pushing the left shoulder round and under the chin. Note the difference: you can't do this without also affecting the right shoulder as well, and forcing it up and round. This observation is a massive breakthrough point in our pursuit of a classic swing!

Figure 15 is a drawing of an unfolded four-bone base, but the practicality is the same. The whole first rod base will move round correctly if the action is one of being pushed round from the left shoulder-blade, but any attempt to pull the base round by retracting the right shoulder-blade will be a total disaster, as to do this will immediately break the constant width of the base: the right shoulder will be able to move round on its own, and leave the left side behind. Such a swing is now irretrievably lost as a classic style swing. *The point to remember is that independent right side shoulder-blade action at the start of the golf swing produces a damaging swing action. Left side shoulder-blade control and action is good.*

However, having said this, it is also equally important that the left shoulder-blade's pushing action is not impeded by an immobile or resisting right shoulder-blade.

Figure 14 shows the completed backswing turn with an intact base almost facing the target. One just has to look at it to see the fully turned base.

2) The constant length of the first rod

The second constant of the triangular first rod is its length. This is maintained by the two arms, acting in a cross-body balanced action and reaction arrangement. On the backswing, from the classic "Reverse K" style set-up, the constant length of the first rod will be maintained by the straight (but not necessarily ram-rod rigid) left arm (Fig. 9, coloured in red). While the backswing progresses, the right arm (both the wrist, elbow and shoulder joints) must remain relaxed and flex, in order to accommodate, and in no way impede, the turning base. On the downswing, the right arm will begin to straighten, and, by impact, both arms will be straight. On the follow-through the right arm will be the one that remains straight, while the left arm relaxes and begins to fold. By these two arm cross-body balanced movements, the constant length of the first rod is maintained.

3) A fully united and integrated grip or hinge

The third constant of the triangular-shaped first rod is the hinge, the union of the two hands at the apex of the triangle. Obviously, they must act as a perfect cross-body fusion of both hands and wrists. However, the left wrist and hand will be the dominant pair during the backswing movement, while the right hand and wrist relax and accommodate to its controlling action. The grip that has been formed at the address position does not alter its position on the club throughout the whole swing action; it merely acts and reacts between the left and right hand throughout the swing movement. The left will control the backswing movement, while the right will relax. On the downswing, both hands will combine as one powerful wrist action, to provide the powerful wrist and forearm whipping into the impact area with both power and precision.

Combining the vertical unit's Support and Rotation with that of the base of the Flail Unit

Let's reflect a little bit on where we have got to. It must be becoming increasingly clear that any classic style golf swing must require a total cross-body skeletal action, both the left and right sides of the skeleton working in harmony. Because of this requirement, it follows that the cross-body connection areas must be the most important areas to concentrate on. Areas such as spinal rotation, or keeping one's two feet in contact with the ground throughout the swing, are simple and easy enough to understand and enact. But this is definitely not the case with the cross-body first rod mechanism. For a start, it has to be constructed carefully each and every time we grip the club. Thereafter, it has to continue working in a cross-balanced fashion throughout the whole swing process. If we fail to achieve either of these, a classic golf swing cannot be achieved. As our shoulder-blade base is the only link we possess between our upper body and our two arms, we simply have to get the action of this link absolutely correct each and every time we swing.

What this boils down to is that obtaining the initial skeletal formation is an absolute must, but just as important is achieving the correct subsequent cross-body muscular action. These are the two most important keys to achieving a sound and repetitive golf swing.

Let's move on a bit. One may ask, where does one start the golf swing? My personal feeling is that it is best done as I have described it by using the "one-piece/one width shoulder rotation takeaway". We have also learnt that this movement is best achieved by being regarded as a left shoulder/arm/club controlled action. If we can achieve this, we are now in business.

Once the initial movement of allowing the two shoulder-blade base to take up its initial "slackness" (its thirty to forty degrees of independent movement), from that point on, the upper chest must start its rotatory movement, and that rotary movement will continue down the spine, pelvis and the upper legs and down to the knees. The knees are the lower limit of the active body and leg rotation, and any further attempt at rotation must be resisted by the lower legs from the knees down to the two feet remaining in firm contact with the ground throughout the backswing - and the early part of the downswing (Fig. 16).

With the two shoulder-blade base working correctly, the right arm relaxed and the left arm firm, the first rod will

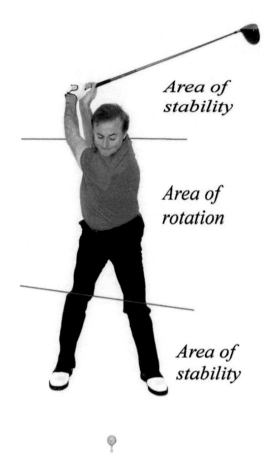

Area of stability

Area of rotation

Area of stability

Figure 16 The full backswing. The areas of stability and the area of rotation

have remained as an intact unit, and the wrists can go ahead with forming both the swing plane and the flail angle. The skeletal mechanics of the backswing are now completed as shown in Fig. 16. There should now be a firm, wound-up skeletal and muscular unit, extending from the two feet on the ground to the grip on the club.

The movement of the downswing must start from the ground and lower legs and knees. Acting together, they will pull the pelvic area back round, followed by the spine, and then the chest. This upper chest movement will automatically carry round with it the fully-wound two-shoulder-blade base of the first rod, and so trigger off the two-rod flail action. The wrists will hold the flail angle at first, but then release the club shaft (second rod) around half way down; the two wrists and forearms will come together in harmony, and assist the developing shoulder centrifugal force to summate the final whip-in (and almost throwing away) of the club-head into and through the ball. The whole skeletal movement is then carried on into a balanced end of swing position.

In carrying out these classic backswing and downswing movements, the skeletal units of the spine, the legs, the two arms and two shoulder-blades have acted in a completely cross-body balanced action and reaction movement. There has been no suggestion of either left or right-side bias in any part of the golf swing movement. The stance and set-up has been perfectly balanced from the ground up, and one actually sees this aspect being carefully set up by the professionals, as they move from one foot to the other in their initial set-up position, seeking a perfect left/right balance. They are also very aware of the triangular first rod being a unified, whole and integrated unit. The head has stayed in the same position in space, and the spine has rotated round a central axis. The base of the first rod of the flail unit rotates round as an intact base, because the two shoulder-blades have moved round in harmony. The two arms suspended from the shoulder-blades have acted and reacted as one centralised rod. The flail hinge angle has been initiated, controlled and released by the two-handed grip working as a single cross-body unit. All the golf swing actions are of a harmonious functioning skeletal unit, acting in both a vertical and cross-body fashion.

Another point perhaps worth restressing at this juncture is that, as with the primitive flail system, it is important to remember that the proximal end or base of the triangular first rod is the main working area. In other words, the shoulders take precedence over the wrists throughout the backswing and the downswing. The hands should never initiate the swing movement by themselves; they merely form the hinge angle and the swing plane in response to the correct shoulder-turning action on the backswing. Again, they must never initiate the downswing – that's for the lower legs. However, they will assist the powerful whip-in of the clubhead at the ball in the impact area. If the hands and arms do initiate the downswing, all they will do is unwind the body rotation that has been so carefully obtained from a correct backswing action.

Now that we have a fair idea of the mechanical movements required of our skeletal framework, we can move on to understanding about the motivating and controlling forces of our hinges and joints – namely our muscular system. Our muscles control every movement we make, and if we wish for our skeletal movements to end up as a repetitive, fluid, balanced and powerful golf swing, then we must take due note of our individual and unique muscular component; it alone is the factor that will determine the outcome of our golf swing movements.

The Muscular Component, or the Driving Force of our Swing

In the previous two chapters, I have described the skeletal mechanics that take place during the execution of a classic-style golf swing. Now that we are aware of the more important of these mechanical movements, namely, the existence of the three cross-body connecting areas of the feet, the shoulder-blades and the hands. These latter two making up the rather fragile first-rod triangle which has to be self-constructed with each swing. Now it is time to see how our muscular system acts to bring all these swing movements together with the power, balance and grace of the classic golf swing.

Our skeletons are merely an inert collection of joints and hinges that can do nothing regarding the initiation or the carrying through of any movement. They may direct or limit a movement within the flexible range of a particular joint, but that is all. So it is to our muscular component that we must now look if we wish to achieve a balanced, functional, and repetitive golf swing movement.

As our skeleton is made up of two halves, each being a perfect mirror image of the other, and united by the vertical and rotatable spine, it is reasonable to expect that a perfectly balanced mirror-image muscular system would be an essential requirement if we are to undertake anything resembling the cross-body balanced movements of the classic swing.

That is as it ought to be, but, unfortunately for us, it is at this precise point that most of us are badly let down. Imperfect human beings that we are, not all of us inherit a suitable muscular and nervous system that will motivate our bi-lateral muscles into undertaking the balanced movements of a classic and functional golf swing, certainly at the power output we require. *The plain fact is that however well our skeletal framework may be set up initially, if our muscular system fails to act in a balanced, cross-body and centralised fashion, then a balanced and centralised physical movement cannot and will not take place.* We may be given the best positional advice that is available – we may read and attempt to mimic the described and illustrated golf swings of the great players. We may start with a totally perfect-looking address and set-up position and be tutored in slow motion movement through every positional gate on the way throughout the swing. However, if our muscular system, which is controlled by our brain, is not tuned into a balanced cross-body movement then there is no chance at all of our being able to reproduce a classic style golf swing with power and precision.

We may be able to obtain a reasonably acceptable, repetitive and functional strike at a golf ball, and, by practising and perfecting such an imperfect swing movement, we may well be able to play to a medium or even a single-handicap figure. Many of us do! However, the reality is that unless we can produce a balanced left/right side muscular action throughout our swing movements, then we will never be able to reproduce the actions of a classic-style golf swing. Not good news for most of us, but, at this stage, take heart! Not all is lost; there is still plenty of light at the end of the tunnel.

First of all, let's look at those who are the haves and those who are the have-nots of the golfing world. The statistics suggest that, in the population at large, the percentage of right-side-dominant individuals is around sixty-four per cent; the percentage of left-side-dominant individuals amount to some four per cent; while the reasonably well muscularly-balanced group number around thirty-two per cent (Fig. 17).

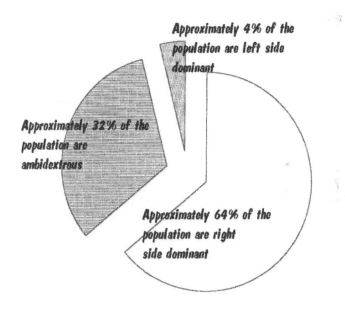

Figure. 17 Likely percentage of the population in the balanced muscular skill areas

It is my belief that it is around this thirty-two per cent of the population that virtually all professional and top amateur athletic sport revolves. This group are the cream of the sporting world as regards potential for a smooth, powerful, precise and unified skeletal movement that can incorporate the whole body as a single functioning unit and they instinctively work around a central axis. As a group these uni-dextrous individuals tend to be drawn towards athletic pursuits, because such movements feel entirely natural to them and they enjoy the execution of such whole body movements.

It is obvious that the divisions between total body balance and right and left-side dominance are grey areas. There has to be shading within each group, and from one group to the next, as to the various degrees of cross-body muscular skills that are available.

However, there is no getting away from the fact that the classic golf swing, in terms of the skeletal movements required, does necessitate that the body musculature functions with both power and almost perfect cross-body control. If such a muscular action happens to be the instinctive and natural function of a person, then the performance of a golf swing will also be a reasonably simple and instinctively balanced action for that individual. It will also be a movement that will not require much conscious thought, and the nearer one is placed towards the centre of the grade of inherited and perfectly cross-balanced muscular function, the more instinctive and powerful a classic golf swing will be. In this respect, many of us may not even be aware of our muscular potential. We may be late-comers to the sporting scene, and, as such, may not have tapped into the full range of muscular skills that we have available. Lucky you, if that is your situation!

From the above statements, it would seem that all top class golfers must be in the broad cross-body balanced group, and most of the better golfers will in all likelihood be towards, or even marginally to the left side, of the central point. Many professionals actually state this in their writings and autobiographies. Sam Snead, the possessor of perhaps the most natural swing ever seen, is a perfect example. As a junior he was unsure whether to play the game right or left-handed; both came equally easily to him. Ben Hogan, Johnny Miller and Bob Charles were the same. David Graham actually changed from left to right. Phil Mickelson is right-handed in everything except golf. Paul Lawrie will sign his autographs with his left hand, but plays golf right handed. We learn that young Tiger Woods actually picked up and swung the club left-handed in the first instance. I would suggest that his father was fortunate indeed that both he and his wife endowed young Tiger with the perfect muscular genes for golf, otherwise their efforts to create a golfing superstar would have been doomed to failure.

And so it goes on; rarely can one find a good right-sided golfer without above average left-side ability, and vice versa, if he or she plays golf left handed. A glance at other sports also support this view, and it is no surprise that cricketers, soccer players and other top sportsmen and women display similar ambidextrous skills. Cricket, in particular, abounds with test and county players who bat right-handed and bowl left, or vice versa: far above the average for any given population.

I suppose it has to be some minor comfort for us to know that it is not really our fault if we are not competent golfers in the lower handicap ranges – it has to be our parents, and ancestors, who are responsible for that!

But don't despair, even though you may feel that you are in the side-dominant muscular range category. If we can learn a bit more about our muscular component and appreciate the areas that fail us most, then, from this knowledge, we ought to be able to go forward and rectify most of our faults.

We have now reached the point where we have answers as to the reasons behind the great variability of golf swings we see on every golf course every day. Although right/left side dominance balance may shade across the broad spectrum of individuals, it would seem that there is a definable point somewhere along the scale where a person is so right-side dominant that it is virtually inevitable that they will clothe their skeletal set-up, however good that may be, with a right-side dominant musculature. If so, that swing is doomed from the outset. The address position may well be anatomically perfect, but if the muscular component is loaded towards a right side bias, it will be a certainty that the very first swing movement will not be a cross-body balanced movement. The base of the first rod of the flail will instantly become disrupted, and, along with this, the whole triangular first rod system. From this point on, the swing is irretrievably set off on completely the wrong path. (The four per cent of left-side-dominant individuals amongst us are in a similar situation to the right-side-dominant players, but are forced by their degree of dominance to play the game left-handed. I will therefore not separate them as a separate category, as they will have precisely the same problems as the right-side individuals, but in reverse.)

Now for some good news. If a golfer is able, perhaps artificially, to manufacture a well-balanced left/right musculature at the address position, then there is every chance that the two shoulder-blades will start the swing movement in harmony, that the triangular first-rod mechanism will remain intact, and that a classic style swing will take place.

So, the problem the majority of higher handicap golfers want answers to, is, how do I move from a handicap style swing towards a classic style? This is the very problem which I had as a youth.

Before going on to answer this massive, but not insurmountable, question, let's have a look at the well-balanced group first of all, as it is certainly not all plain sailing for them. They also have their problems, minor though they may be compared to those facing the handicap golfer. Even in this favoured group of individuals, there will be some who will tend towards either right or left-side dominance. Those tending towards right-side dominance will always have slightly more problems than those tending towards the left, especially if they go for extra power. If they do this, there is always the possibility that their right side may on occasions take too much control, and upset the critical cross-body balance in the shoulder/arm/grip triangle area, and result in a wayward shot. We see this fairly often where professionals try to pour on full power in order to reach a long par five hole in two shots. Most pros do appreciate that it is a far more profitable exercise to attempt to work at eighty to eighty-five per cent of their power for most of the time. But every now and again, it is perhaps worth the gamble of going for broke, although the number of wayward shots we see demonstrates that they do lose out on many occasions.

Many amongst the favoured group of golfers have had excellent professional careers, and have earned vast amounts of money on the golfing circuits of the world; but they sometimes develop a personal bug about needing more power or perhaps obtaining better control or flight of the ball. Rarely do they succeed. It may work reasonably well for them on the practice ground, but not with any consistency on the course, where they are under much more stressful competitive conditions. My feeling is that, in attempting to improve their swing, they have actually moved marginally away from the unique muscular balance that has served them so well in the past, and they have now introduced a slight conflict between their skeletal mechanics and their muscular instincts, a conflict that did not exist before. The number of golfers who eventually find this out and then try to return to their old swings is legion; we can all think of many recent examples. Some make it back; many don't. It is also this problem that makes a wise coach hesitate to embark on any swing changes for a golfer whom he may have coached, with success, for many years.

On the other hand, there is a group of talented but unfortunate players who may have inherited an excellent muscular component but who are forced into seeking an alteration in their swing mechanics in order to cope with a damaged skeletal system. I suppose the perfect example of this has to be Tiger Woods. Because of the damage to his skeletal system, he has been forced into adopting a mechanical swing change (designed to "play away" from the nerve pain caused by his back injury, we are told). I have no doubt that this will be slightly alien to his natural muscular instincts, and, in order to accomplish this, he will have mentally to override his inborn muscular instincts, and rein them in, to a degree. He has had little choice but to take this path in order to reduce the stress on his damaged joints and ligaments. I am sure that if he could keep performing at this new level and staying at around eighty per cent of the power level he had before, he could have many more years of, shall we say, less competitive golf. However, Tiger being Tiger, and such a determined character, from what I saw prior to his last breakdown, it seems that it is almost impossible for him to stop trying to compete when his younger partners are thumping the ball so many yards past him. Sadly, I fear that it must almost be a case of accepting what he has, and joining the slightly shorter hitters, or opting out. (I wrote this in 2016, and, from recent events, it would seem that we are going to witness a further competitive attempt with his now fused lumbar spine. So far, things are working well, but time alone will tell.)

But back to the main theme of the book - our handicap swing problems. The look at the skeletal mechanics has been useful, as we have been able to identified the two major skeletal units, each with their differing tasks. The vertical unit is simple enough: it provides centralised support and rotation, and must function in a balanced cross-body fashion through the two feet stationed on the ground and the head remaining at a fixed point in space. The first rod of the flail unit is a much more complex problem; it requires the triangle of bones to be re-formed prior to every swing, and then made to act as if it were one single mid-line rod. Only perfect cross-body muscular balance (or slightly left-side-dominated) can achieve this for us.

So let's move on to the next chapter, and look at how the vast majority of higher handicap golfers might go about modifying their instinctive, but faulty muscular component towards one that is in harmony with a classic-style golf swing.

Starting to Put it All Together

I mentioned in my introduction to the book that my role is not that of a hands-on teacher of the golf swing; that is for the trained experts, and, in my opinion, everyone would be well-advised to use their services. My aim in writing this small volume is to explain the reasons that I believe lie behind the immense variety of average-to-poor swings that we see on golf courses every day. Most of these swings are far removed from any resemblance to a classic golf swing. Furthermore, they fail to be either consistent, powerful or accurate. If the conclusions which I have reached in this book happen to be of assistance to club professionals in their teaching, or to swell their number of customers, I will be absolutely delighted. However, my main aim is to reassure the struggling higher-handicap golfers that their inability to produce a classic-style swing has a causation; it is explicable, it is understandable, and it is open to remedial action. I hope this will encourage these handicap players to make use of this new knowledge, as it does open up new avenues for them to improve dramatically. It will certainly be more difficult for some than for others, but action on this knowledge must surely be the path to aim for, with the almost certain prospect of a better swing, and a downward trend in one's handicap.

It is a well-recognised fact that what we think we are doing, and what we actually do, are often poles apart; and it is for this reason that I feel that professional guidance, along with better understanding by the pupil of the problems which they are up against, has to be the best and quickest way forward to achieving a rapid improvement. But, if it has to be self-taught tuition from the written word or videos, then I am quite certain that the contents of this book will also prove to be of immense value in achieving a much improved swing technique.

So let's reflect on where we have got to. The permanent and unalterable links across our two skeletal halves are the central spine and the oval-shaped pelvic bones supporting our two legs. It is simple enough to make these links act across the mid-line. However, this is not so with the other three mechanical cross-body links, and we now know that inherited cross-body muscular imbalance has its damaging effect across these three links. These links are the soles of the feet through the ground, the grip of the two hands, and the muscular cross-body links between the two shoulder blades. These are the three crucial areas we must concentrate on now.

Every fit and healthy, even if side-dominant, individual, ought to be able to work their muscles in a balanced and cross-body fashion at slow speed. However, problems arise when speed and power is added to the equation. The more side-dominant one is, the more severe will be the problems; and my feeling is that there is a cut-off point at which the task may be too difficult to overcome.

What proportion this may be of the sixty-eight per cent of side-dominant individuals in the population, I have no idea, it will depend very much on each individual's aims and ambitions. My guess is that it may well be around half of the group of side-dominant golfers. This group may well decide that pursuing a classic-style golf swing is really not worth the effort, and that they would be better off sticking with a golf swing that feels more comfortable and natural for them. They know it will never be a classic swing, but it will be a swing that provides more enjoyable, tension-free golf for them, and, in the end, is likely to be a better option than attempting to chase a classic-style swing.

If the decision is to leave well alone and stay with a swing that feels entirely natural, yet at the same time to appreciate that it is not, and never will be, a classic-style golf swing, then at least this decision can now be taken with the knowledge that you have understood the alternatives, and you have made your decision based on facts. If such a decision is taken, then I say 'good luck to you!' You can do this with the comforting knowledge that there are many hundreds of thousands of medium and even upper-single-figure-handicap golfers with such swings – a sort of regular irregular swing becomes your aim. The big advantage of doing this is that such a swing will match with your natural muscular ability and instincts. If this is to be the approach, then such a swing is likely to get a reasonably steady handicap job done. It is a swing that is unlikely to ever show any serious progression downward in one's handicap. Professional golf tutors are faced with this sort of problem every day of their lives, and such golfers are the bread and butter of their working day. Repetition, and a firm foundation for the base of the flail system, become the main aims, rather than any attempt at upper and lower cross-body balance. Certainly, achieving such an aim will go a long way towards a functional but unorthodox golf swing, and will give many higher handicap golfers satisfaction on the course, and much enjoyment when playing with friends. A few further thoughts about this entirely sensible approach later.

However, if the wish is to try for a classic-style swing then I believe the basic problem must now be addressed, namely, that of being a golfer in possession of two variables, neither of which will match with the other. In other words, the possession of a muscular component that is wired into a side-dominant muscular action, yet at the same time being told by all the pundits to enact movements that are totally alien to one's natural muscular instincts. It is a massive problem to overcome, but I hope we can go a long way down this path over the course of the rest of this chapter and the next.

The way forward for this large group of golfers must be to undertake a conscious and deliberate decision to modify one's muscular component towards a balance that will match with the required skeletal swing movements. It will be utterly useless to persist with an instinctive side-dominant muscular balance, in the hope that it may eventually be effective. Neither is there any chance of attempting to increase the control of the weaker side of the body to match with that of the stronger side. Unilateral exercise may well make the weaker side more powerful, but the problem is rather more subtle than that; it is one of cross-body control rather than power. I believe the problem must be approached by bringing the dominant side down a few notches to match with that of the weaker side, thereby achieving the necessary cross-body control and the awareness of just what a balanced total-body action entails, and what it feels like. It is the balanced linking across the feet and the upper body, and within the triangular first rod of the flail unit, that must be the aim. Once one has understood and achieved this balance, then it may be possible to consider the power aspect of the weaker side.

It is not an unreasonable analogy to think of the body musculature as being that of a twin-engine aircraft with one engine rotating its propeller faster than the other, yet without any way of increasing the speed of the weaker engine. As a result, the plane will keep turning towards the weaker side. You can put a more powerful engine on the weaker side, but if it can't rotate the propeller any faster it is not much use. To get such a plane to fly straight, the best solution will be to reduce the speed of the faster engine to match that of the slower one, then the plane will fly straight and true. So, I believe, it is with the human body; one must learn to reduce the control of the dominant side to match that of the less well controlled side, only by doing this will there be any chance of obtaining, and then keeping, a satisfactory cross-body mechanical action across the three important links, and producing a classic-style golf swing action. Of course, in a plane one may play about with the rudder and the ailerons and obtain a constant heading, in a rather crab-like fashion. In fact, this is precisely what the side-dominant players do; they destroy the smooth streamlined mechanics, in an attempt to keep a steady heading. Such an approach brings about loss of speed, and requires constant tinkering to keep a steady heading.

I will devote the rest of this chapter to my thoughts as to how every side-dominant individual might start to move towards a balanced muscular component, and therefore, a swing movement that is in tune with the accepted style of golf swing, incidentally, in so doing, giving themselves a much better chance to gain maximum benefit from any professional tuition they may undertake.

Professionals have always insisted that the foundation of learning the golf swing must be to obtain a classic stance, grip and posture. I couldn't agree more; this, indeed, has to be the correct starting point for everyone wishing to perform a near-classic golf swing, so let's start there. From this decision and its implementation, the next important move (although rarely stated) must be to clothe that framework with a correctly matching muscular component. If one is right-side-dominant, this means that one simply has to learn to relax the whole of the right-side musculature from the shoulder to the lower right leg in order to get anywhere near the mental awareness of what good cross-body balance actually feels like. And perhaps one must go even further and actually have one's left side in control of the start of the golf swing movement. I suggest that the easiest way is to take your stance, then relax the whole right side, and undertake the golf swing with the left arm alone. This is not with any intention of perfecting the full swing movement at this stage, but merely to get the feel of what a balanced cross-body shoulder and leg movement (i.e. two of the three important cross-body connections) is actually like when the more powerful right arm and right side is taken out of the equation and the left arm remains in absolute control of the backswing movement - and the first part of the downswing.

So we must start this "left arm alone" swing with what feels like a well-balanced stance, with both feet flat on the ground and only the left hand holding the club (maybe use a short, weighted indoor practise club, a lighter short iron, or even go well down the grip of your driver). Relax, don't hunch at the shoulders, stand tall, and let the two shoulders feel as if they are "a bit lax and droopy" and are suspended from the mid-line back of the neck. In other words, try and become aware of your two shoulder-blades with the upper arms extending down from them – keep both shoulders relaxed, but with only the left hand holding the club. Keep the left arm itself almost vertically down, and make sure both feet remain balanced and flat on the ground throughout the swing movement. Keep both knees bent with the knees to feet feeling active and supportive of the body and left arm above. Make absolutely sure that the right shoulder, right arm and elbow stay completely relaxed, and take no active part in (nor impede in any way) the pending backswing movement.

Be aware of the straight left arm from the left shoulder to the back of the left hand, as if it were a single unit. From this initial balanced stance, it is useful if the first move is a slight forward press with the back of the left hand, with the left shoulder acting as the pivot or hinge of the straight first rod. It will be the instinctive muscular rebound action from this minor forward press that will initiate the rotation movement from the left shoulder as it starts off under the chin and into the two-shoulder-blade-turning "one-piece takeaway" movement. Keep concentrating, and be aware of the back of the left hand and the left shoulder as being at either end of a unified and straight first rod. The instant the movement starts, let the back of the left hand start to rotate and find the swing plane; and, at the same time, let the wrist hinge as it starts to develop the flail angle. The right arm, shoulder and body must continue to do absolutely nothing but relax and not impede the left-side-controlled shoulder movements. As the left shoulder starts to move down and round the chest wall, the relaxed right shoulder will be shoved back and up round the upper back of the neck. The thirty to forty degrees of independent shoulder-blade movement, relative to the chest, is quickly taken up, and the base of the first rod is now firmly connected to the top of the chest wall, with the two main skeletal units welded together as one.

To obtain further turning movement, the whole upper chest must now start to rotate round (still being pushed from the left shoulder). The upper chest and spine will continue to rotate and carry along with it, the two shoulder-blade base of the flail unit. As the upper chest and body turning continues, the legs, from the knees down to the two firm feet flat on the ground, will, and must, start to resist the upper body rotary movement. The weight will shift towards the right hip and leg. Let it; but don't try to get more tuning by lifting the left heel off the ground. Ensure that all the body and chest rotation only takes place between the three points of the two knees below, and the (stable point in space) of the back of the neck spine above (Fig. 18). Keep centralised body rotation with the body weight staying between the two feet, and with the head facing forward. It is a useful check to keep being mentally aware of these three boundary points during the whole of the backswing. The flexed knees will obviously move in response to the body's turning, but to all intents and purposes they must act as the buffers or resistors to the chest, body, pelvic and thigh rotation occurring above them.

Try this "left arm alone" swing over and over again, until you can appreciate and retain the sensation you get from a left-side-controlled start to the backswing, along with a full upper chest turn and the firm tension loading of the lower legs.

Figure. 18. The left arm alone swing. Getting the cross-body feet and the left shoulder working

Another concept of initiating the left-arm-alone backswing is to execute the same forward press, but then start the swing with the right hip making the initial backward rotation. This movement tends to give the feeling that one is then dragging the left shoulder and straight left arm back and under the chin. It perhaps also helps to accentuate the feeling of a relaxed right arm and shoulder area. Many pros do appear to do this starting move rather than the two-shoulder-controlled one-piece takeaway as their first move. I have an open mind on this one, but feel that, at this stage, it might be more beneficial to start with the shoulder-initiated one-piece takeaway movement, and to help to establish it early on that the main working area is to be the left shoulder, not the right hand, and never, ever, the right shoulder.

Keep repeating this backswing, with your two feet remaining flat on the ground throughout both the backswing and the initial part of the downswing. Obtain the powerful feeling of the trunk and upper back muscles being stretched and primed, as the back of the chest turns towards the hole. Be aware of the left and right lower legs' muscles being stretched and prepared for the return swing action. The old description of "swinging in a barrel" is a very apt phrase, and the right hip area feels like the back-stop to the turning process. As the backswing progresses towards its end, it becomes obvious that the lower legs, acting together, simply have to be the springboard for the initiation of the return action.

This left-arm-alone golf swing (right arm if you play left-handed) demonstrates just what good cross-body balanced action between the upper chest and two feet feels like, and likewise across the two shoulder-blades. The only missing cross-body component in this style of practice swing is the third link, the one between the two hands. Despite this, the left-arm swing is an excellent replica of a full backswing action, and serves as a powerful reminder that the right shoulder, the right upper arm and the right elbow are *not required to do any active work during the backswing movement.* In fact, the main duty of the right shoulder, right arm and indeed the whole right side, at this stage of the swing, is to avoid causing any obstruction to the left-arm-controlled backswing movement. The period for action of the right arm and right side will come in the latter part of the downswing movement.

The thing to appreciate as you carry out the swing is that the whole backswing movement can be as leisurely, as slow and as stress-free as you like. Doing it the way we have done gives sense and meaning to the often-quoted phrases from the class players: they do not grip the club shaft with an excessively powerful grip, they take their time to develop the backswing, and they have plenty of time to pause at the top if they so wish. All these points are made meaningful by using the left arm/left shoulder backhanded takeaway.

Now let's turn to the downswing. It becomes obvious that the lower legs below the knees have to be the springboard for the downswing. Their powerful start to the downswing will de-rotate the hips, the torso and the chest; this powerful action will pull the upper chest back towards the address position, and, by so doing, trigger the tightly-wound two-shoulder base of the first rod of the flail unit. In our one-arm swing, it is only the straight left arm that is acting as the sole first rod; but even here, one does get a good concept of the unleashing of the two-rod flail, with its centrifugal force being exerted on the club shaft, and encouraging the whip-in of the clubhead at the ball. Where is the actual starting point for the downswing? Certainly in the lower legs; and, as you practice the left arm swing, you will soon get a feel for the powerful start to the downswing. Some say the left heel, some say the left hip, are pulled back; most say that the two knees and lower legs act in unison. All are necessary; it just depends which one, or maybe all together, work for you. I personally like the concept of the left hip pulling straight back and forming a good firm left-side skeletal post (from heel to shoulder) for the flail action to be braced against, as it whips through the ball.

I remember being told to "throw your ass at the target." Not very elegant language, but a perfectly reasonable concept! Just visualise Rory McIlroy's left side hitting position, and you have got the idea.

One of the dangers of the left-arm swing is that it becomes very easy to break the left elbow in an attempt to get the clubhead further back and round, so do try and keep the left arm straight throughout the backswing, and make the back muscles and the upper chest and body do the main rotary work.

One appreciates that, in the left-arm swing, the hitting area tends to become more of a weak pulled sweep of the clubhead past the ball, rather than a firmly-controlled and powerful whip into and through the ball. This is because the flail hinge, with only the left arm functioning, is a physically weak link, and it is at this point that we require the right forearm and right wrist action to come to its assistance.

The fact that, whatever your side dominance may be, the cross-balanced movements of our chest body and legs come relatively easily to us is because we tend to practice such movements every day of our lives. We may well have a dominant right leg, and we will always use this leg for preference if we kick a ball. However, the very act of using balanced cross-body movements of our legs and body occurs every day of our lives, in exercises such as walking, running, jumping, climbing stairs or whatever; such exercise continually exercises the cross-body balanced movements between our two legs and body. Not so with our shoulder-blade and arm movements. If we are right-side-dominant, we will instinctively prefer to use our right hand, our arm and our right shoulder for every possible function. Obviously, we can all use our left arm, but because it has a considerably reduced degree of control, we tend not to bother. So it is with the golf swing of almost every right-side dominant golfer; they tend to use their right shoulder, right arm and right hand as the major controlling force for all their golf swing movements. It is at this point that virtually all higher-handicap golfers go astray. Start with a right-side-dominant musculature at the set-up position, and a handicap swing is inevitable. I feel this left-arm-alone swing technique is perhaps the only way to understand and get used to the required feeling of a left-side-controlled cross-body shoulder action.

Once one has become used to the left shoulder, left arm and back of the left hand initiating the swing, it is easy to experiment with varying the techniques of a strong left hand grip, a weak grip, a vertically down left arm, an angled-forward left arm, and the extent of the flail angle at the top of the swing. Each variation will have its effect on the swing plane and the flail angle. As we all differ in our skeletal ratios, there is no one answer to the best set-up position, and it is here that expert advice can be so helpful.

Once one is aware of the importance of left-side muscular control in the triggering of the correct cross-body controlled backswing, now is the time to tentatively introduce the right-hand grip into the equation. Keep the right shoulder and elbow joints relaxed, and not interfering in any way with the backswing movement; maybe just put the thumb and first finger on the grip initially. Get the feeling that *it is only the right side wrist and right forearm* that is relevant to the action, and this occurs as the closing flail angle between the left arm and the club shaft is whipped into a straight line at the point of contact with the ball. As the sequence and degree of cross-body muscular balance becomes clearer, one can move more towards the conventional grip, and, perhaps for the first time ever, appreciate just what is required of a good cross-body balanced golf swing.

In the next chapter, using the knowledge and the muscular feeling we have gained from acting out the left-arm swing movement, we can now try and assimilate this slow-motion swing without any ball contact into a fully-fledged swing that has some resemblance to a classic-style golf swing, and will strike the ball with reasonable power and accuracy.

Putting the Theory into Practice for Side-Dominant Golfers

Figure. 19 Horizontal test-bed swing

I have made the point that right-side-dominant individuals tend to use their right leg, hand or arm for virtually every possible action - even though it might be better carried out by the left side. It is exceedingly difficult for such individuals to bring their left arm or hand into any action, unless it is almost an emergency situation. Many sports can be played quite happily with the right hand in control, indeed with the whole right side in almost total command – all the racquet games, cricket, hockey, darts, football, and even the short game in golf. So there is little doubt that it is not going to be an easy task to adapt to a new style of golf swing that brings the left hand, left arm and left shoulder into the swing movement, often as the dominant partner in the backswing and the lower left leg area in the start of the downswing.

However, using the left-arm-alone swing, we have been able to accomplish a feeling and understanding of the cross-body balance and function of the shoulder-blades and the feet. We have also been able to appreciate that the two shoulder-blades are the working hub of the two-rod flail action.

To better groove the action that the shoulders and hands execute, I suggest that we move away from the conventional golf set-up, and instead address an imaginary ball at about mid-chest height, with, as near as possible, a Reverse K set-up (Fig. 19). This set-up position has the advantage of unwinding and separating the two main skeletal units, and making it much easier to identify and perform the correct cross-body actions of the two units while they are separated entities.

In setting up for this test-bed swing keep the spine straight with the derrière protruding and the knees bent, giving oneself a good firm and balanced base, with both feet flat on the ground (not up on one's toes) and with a feeling of being strong and firm from the knees down. The grip should be taken with the palms of the hands facing each other and almost vertical. Keep an angle of some fifteen degrees (or one hundred and sixty-five degrees) between the arms and club, with the club-head at around shoulder height and the grip some six inches below. Now relax both shoulder-blades, and feel that the arms are evenly suspended from the mid-line back of the neck. Use a normal two-arm set-up, with the left arm straight and the right elbow and shoulder areas completely relaxed, and the grip united with both hands in a normal grip, but with the most powerful part of the grip, at this stage, being the last three fingers of the left hand, maintaining a firm grip on the club and making the left arm from the left shoulder to the back of the left hand feel in control - just as was done in the left-arm-alone swing.

So we are now in the Reverse K address position moved up to a horizontal plane, perfectly balanced between both feet and with the right shoulder, elbow, arm and right side relaxed, but with a comfortably united grip. One of the big advantages of this horizontal shoulder/arm swing position is that the swing plane is accurately defined for us; it is the near-horizontal plane, as defined by our straight left arm. The clubhead is slightly outside (above) the swing plane, as determined by our fifteen-degree angle, and, because of this, the left wrist will have a slightly cupped wrist angle. At first, do everything in ultra-slow motion. Start the swing with the left shoulder/arm/ back of the left hand in control, forward press (or pull the left hip back a fraction) just as in the one-arm swing, and carry out the left-shoulder-led one-piece takeaway (Fig. 20). Merge it into the full upper chest, spinal and pelvic turning movement, keeping the turning between the two planes of the neck spine above down to the knees below. Keep concentrating on the swing plane and the developing flail angle throughout the backswing, and try and keep the clubhead on the horizontal plane. Ignore the right shoulder, elbow and arm; just let them stay totally relaxed, and going along for the ride. At this point, the backswing should feel much like it did for the one-arm swing. A properly relaxed right arm will fold in at the elbow, and will keep the right shoulder quiet and not in any way impeding the left arm and hand grip controlled takeaway of the two-shoulder base of the first rod. Keep the head facing forward; don't let it come round with the shoulder turning. You are now at the top of the backswing, and have defined the swing plane, developed the flail angle, and flexed the upper arm joints

Figure. 20 The one-piece takeaway movement in the horizontal swing

fully. Meanwhile, the two feet must have remained flat on

the ground (Fig. 21). All much the same feeling that you had with the one arm swing, but we now have the right hand on the grip, and ready to come into the action on the latter part of the downswing.

Note, in this style of left-controlled slow-motion swing, that, at the end of the backswing, this position can be held quite easily before initiating the returning movement – no need to rush with a great backward and forward movement. Get used to this slow-motion swing rhythm; try to hold the backswing for a short pause, and make sure it is the lower legs that initiate the downswing.

The return or downswing starts with exactly the same feel as with the left-arm-alone swing, and, as I said before, some feel that they initiate it with the left heel, others with the left hip, yet others with both knees. Come what may, it is the whole left-side skeletal framework from the left heel to the left shoulder that virtually snaps the left hip backwards into a rigid structure from heel to shoulder, and, by so doing, immediately contracts the wound-up power of the muscles of the thighs and trunk. This works rapidly up the body and spine, and pulls the upper chest back towards the address position. Along with it must come the two shoulder-blades, i.e. the base of the first rod of the flail unit. At last the right side is now starting to play its main role in the action. The united grip now comes in, with powerful right finger and thumb, right wrist and lower right forearm muscular control assisting the hinge action between the first and second rods, with the feeling that the two arms and the club are being extended or thrown away from the shoulders. At the imaginary impact point, the left arm and club shaft will be in a straight line, and the right arm will also be straight. After impact, the movement will quite naturally go on into the follow-through, as the left elbow starts to fold.

If one is very right-side-dominant, it will take a bit of time to get used to the movements brought about by both the one-arm swing and the horizontal swing, and the new feeling of the swing's being worked from the shoulders, and not the hands. However, before moving the horizontal swing towards ground level and trying it with a ball, I suggest that one goes on a bit further with the horizontal swing, and experiments by introducing a few faults and observing their effects. For instance, once you have got to a good horizontal wound-up backswing position, try starting the downswing by pulling back with the right hand in command. Just see what a disaster this is! If the right arm or hand starts the downswing action, it is almost as if a catapult that is primed ready for a sling shot is released by pushing the catapult itself backwards. All the pent-up and stretched muscle power is instantly lost. So it will be with the golf swing; to get to the top of the swing and then to start back again with the right hand is merely to unwind the very same muscles which you have just primed. It simply must be the lower legs that initiate the downswing.

Figure. 21 Full backswing of the horizontal style swing

One can experiment by introducing other faults. Let the cross-body lower leg base break asunder by allowing the left heel to lift right up on the backswing. Note that, if this happens, no thigh and trunk muscles are being stretched; it has in effect allowed the top and the bottom of the muscular body tube to turn as one unit. Result – no wind up, one is forced to start the downswing from the top – that is, either from the hands or from the shoulders, as nothing has been wound in the lower body and legs. Once you get the idea, and the feel, of good cross-body muscular action taking place across the feet, the shoulders and the grip, the correct golf swing movements begin to fall into place and make sense.

Now is the time to start transferring the horizontal swing down towards to the correct ball position on the ground, and repeating exactly the same sequence of movements. Make sure that you really do appreciate the need for the gentle "back of the left shoulder/arm" forward press and the recoil into the initiation of the left-side-controlled one-piece takeaway. I think it was Tom Kite who described this initial movement as being akin to swinging a milk pail on the end of a piece of rope (the rope being from the left shoulder to the clubhead). This is a good analogy for the concept of the flail-unit action's being a tension-free controlled left-shoulder movement back and under the chin, independent of the upper chest at first, and then continuing along with the upper chest. Don't rush it, just let the left side start gently into the swing.

From all the above, one can fully understand just why the task of teaching a right-side-dominant golfer is not, and never will be, a simple half-hour job. A movement that one has instinctively used for perhaps more years than one may care to remember will be difficult indeed to alter in a single session. In my view, it needs the pupil to understand fully the aims and the pitfalls that they face; then constructive action can follow. It just has to be knowledge of the situation first; remedial action can then follow this understanding.

I believe that the horizontal swing technique reveals just about all there is to know about the basic mechanics of the classic style golf swing, and how the muscular actions of the three vitally important cross-body connections between our two skeletal halves are set-up, how their movements are controlled, and how the power is delivered at the correct point in the swing arc.

I have described all the skeletal movements almost as if they were done by numbers; but this is not so. There still remains plenty of scope for individual variations. We all differ in our body build; some of us are short and plump, some are tall and thin. Some of us are extremely flexible in our joint movements, others are more limited. Each variant will tend to leave its imprint on an individual's swing pattern. In this respect, I have already mentioned the differing initiating movements of the swing. Jack Nicklaus has always stated that both the backswing and downswing start from below. Others are equally adamant that the backswing starts from the shoulders. It matters little, provided that, at the end of the backswing, the same cross-body muscles are stretched and prepared to initiate the downswing.

Again, on the downswing, some golfers may emphasise the wrist action, others the leg action, while others may be poetry in motion throughout. All will look different, but all will deliver a good end result when the clubface strikes the ball.

Apart from the differences due to body build and muscular emphasis, there are many other individual deviations from the classic concepts that have been extremely successful; for example, the rather off-beat swing planes of Jim Furyk, and, in former times, those of Amon Darcy and Gay Brewer. There are also the excessive foot movements of Bubba Watson. They all appear to go against any rigidly strict interpretation of a correct classic swing; however, all these players have been very successful in their careers. The important point is that all these players must have an inner compensatory mechanism built into them, which allows them to adjust and arrive at the point of impact in a perfectly controlled and classical bottom of the swing position.

These few observations only serve to strengthen my view that anyone starting to play golf or wishing to improve their existing swing technique would be well advised to go to their professional for observation of their address position, the sequence of their movements and the plane of their swing. However, if they go with the understanding of what cross-body muscular balance entails, how it can be enacted and what the main pitfalls are likely to be, then the progress under expert guidance ought to be satisfying and pleasurable.

Now that we have got the actual mechanical movements, along with awareness of the importance of the three important cross-body areas, and how they act, let's now have a few thoughts on our approach to each new round of golf.

A few Random Thoughts on Pre-play Routines

Let's say you have developed your new, near-classic-style, golf swing. You have spent hours on the practice ground or range; you have discovered the vital role that the shoulders play in linking together the two main skeletal units; and you are now ready to put things to the test on the course. What's the best approach before you strike your opening shot on the first tee? In virtually all active sports, players tend to practise a few routines to limber up before the actual game starts. Golf is no exception, and perhaps we can take some indications from what the pros themselves get up to in their pre-play routines. They will first of all hit shots throughout the whole range of their clubs, then spend time on the short game area and the putting green. Most of us do not have such facilities, nor the time. So I suggest that a minimum effort ought to be a few "shadow-boxing routines" - along with a short spell on the putting green, if available.

What is the best routine? I feel that the principal aim must be to exercise and re-familiarise ourselves with the correct muscular functioning of the three important cross-body connections; they really do hold the key to reproducing a classic- style golf swing. If you are right-side-dominant, your "faulty" inborn control will not go away; so you will continually need to refresh the necessity for left-side shoulder control of the backswing, along with a relaxed right side that will not interfere, nor take over control of the initial swing movements. As you take your address position, make sure that you really do have an evenly balanced base, with both feet flat on the ground, and your right side relaxed. Then I suggest a routine of perhaps half a dozen left-hand-alone swings in order to check that the two important cross-body connections are functioning well: namely, that the left shoulder is starting the one-piece takeaway and thereafter going on into the full upper-chest turning movement as the left arm crosses the mid-line under the chin. Secondly, that the feet stay balanced and in contact with the ground throughout the backswing and the lower legs are fully prepared and primed to initiate the downswing. Aim for a braced left side with the left hip moving back. Try to get a one-two-three – one rhythm established early on. It's all about relaxed shoulders initiating a slow easy rotation of the two shoulder-blade base of the first rod turning mechanism and being aware of the cross-body muscular feel you are aiming for. Concentrate on keeping all the active rotation within the three point boundaries of the back of the neck above and the two knees below.

After this left side one-arm priming routine, switch to the horizontal swing, and introduce a relaxed right arm, right shoulder, right elbow and right hand grip into the equation. Don't let the right side take over the initial moves – nor impede them. The left arm and shoulder must be in control at the address position, and throughout the backswing. Establish the feel of your swing plane early on in the takeaway (horizontal in this case). Make sure that the club face goes from vertical at address to horizontal on the way back, then return to vertical at the hitting point and to vertically down thereafter. I suggest keeping the right finger and thumb grip fairly light at first, but, as you gradually move the swing plane down to the ball position, you can strengthen the grip as you establish the feel of the arms extending down from the shoulders, and the right wrist and forearm controlling the whipping-in role, as you reach the impact point. Continue to keep uppermost in your mind the three points of the two knees below and the back of the neck spine above; and make sure that all the active body rotation stays within these two planes. That's all that should be necessary, less than five minutes of your time before you step confidently on to the first tee and *ease* the ball away.

One sees the professionals practising in miniature the cross-body actions of the shoulders, the body-turning action and the sequences of the downswing action. They do it over and over again on the tee, prior to striking the ball. The basic ingredients required are all there in this relaxed, slow-motion, mini-left-arm-and-shoulder controlled swing of no more than half distance, back and forth.

It is of interest to observe a few of the other practice ground routines that some players adopt prior to their tournament rounds. Katayama has one of the strangest of them all; he hits many practice shots right-handed, and then switches round to a left-handed stance, and whacks off another batch of balls left-handed. Quite obviously, he must be a perfectly cross-balanced individual. He must have complete centralised body control as his normal, natural and instinctive muscular movement. His odd routine simply has to be aimed at making sure his cross-body connections are in good working order prior to playing.

Very few of us could adopt his routine. Nevertheless, I have heard of a few amateur golfers who possess both left and right-handed clubs, with a different handicap linked to each set. They have to declare before a medal round which handicap they are playing to on the day. The former England cricket captain, Brian Close, was one such player, with both handicaps in low single figures.

Harrington is another player who sometimes uses a rather strange routine of running a few paces at the ball, and only then releasing the club at the ball. I am not quite sure what this one is about; but I assume that he is making sure that his firm left side is functioning correctly in the hitting zone. Jiménez is another golfer with a fairly unique mini practice swing, which he uses while waiting on the tee. He does his mini practice swing much nearer the horizontal plane than any of the other professionals; it is very similar to the horizontal swing I have described, but perhaps more on the first downward stage towards the ball. It would appear to be his fairly unique way of testing that his three cross-body links are functioning correctly, and that he is fully aware of his intended swing plane.

I once read about a golf instructor who used to get his pupils to run on the spot for a few minutes before starting his lesson. It is a good idea in principle, to get the body functioning as one unit, but I doubt whether it would be very popular with the older generation!

So there it is. If you are a right-side-dominant individual, you simply must take the right-side muscular power down to that of the left side, and, thereafter, prioritise the three important cross-body muscular working areas of the shoulders, the hands and the lower legs, and ensure that the actual rotatory movement is only taking place between the three points of the two knees below and the back of the neck above. Keep thinking of the shoulders as the main working area – never the hands alone.

Most tournament professionals state that they play at only around eighty per cent of their full power, and one can appreciate that this is true, as many of them must be fairly near the periphery of their balanced muscular range; at around eighty per cent of full power, they will instinctively appreciate that they will be more accurate and in better control of the ball at this power ratio. However, the golfers who are on the left side of the ambidextrous range are fortunate indeed, as they can mostly work at their full power if they so wish, and not risk disrupting their swing.

If, like most high-handicap golfers, you are in the right-side-dominant category, then you will always have to work against your natural instincts; and many of us will need considerable determination to curb the occasional urge to give the ball a right good welly. Easing it smoothly away must be the abiding thought. Lash at it once and that will cause right-side-dominant control to take over. If you do it, it will often be extremely difficult to get back into the rhythm during the remainder of that round. The more right-side-dominant one is, the more difficult it will be to play one's best golf in a strong wind, or on a seven-thousand-yard course, or playing against a longer-hitting opponent. Nevertheless, I hope that many more club golfers will now find pleasure in the knowledge of how to go about seeking a near-classic-style swing, and, perhaps more comfortingly, in the thought of knowing how to continually re-discover it, even though an occasional lapse may occur.

As I mentioned earlier, there is a percentage of side-dominant golfers who either can't, because they are so excessively side-dominant, or simply don't want to, spend the time or effort in chasing a classic or near-classic swing. To these golfers, I suggest that their best approach is to quite deliberately pursue a sort of regular-irregular style of golf swing. Let's find out a little more about these so-called deviant and faulty golf swings.

A Few Final Thoughts and Some Observations Regarding "Faulty" Swings

We are all the products of our genetic inheritance, and some of us are better adapted than others to engage in certain sports. Golf is unique amongst sports in that it is really three games in one: the long game, the short game and putting. Each aspect requires slightly different skill characteristics. The long game has the most exacting requirements, because of its emphasis on cross-body muscular balance. The short game and putting are not so demanding and right-side muscular dominance can be quite acceptable. Let's have a look at the reasons why.

The Skills of Pitching and Putting

Pitching – So far my script has been solely concerned with the classic-style swing and the long game. However, in the short game (say from some hundred yards into the flag) there are many higher-handicap club golfers who possess strongly side-dominant swings throughout their game, and, as a result, are inconsistent long game players. Despite this, many of these players are quite capable of holding their own against their lower-handicap brethren as regards their short game skills. The reason for this nearer equality of short game skills is because of the fact that the long and the short game are testing different skill characteristics. The most important requirement for the long game is undoubtedly that of having excellent cross-body balance skills. The short game, however, is quite different, in that it demands excellent hand/eye co-ordination, and much less in the way of cross-body skills. It can be played with one hand dominant or both hands equally, it doesn't matter much; power and balanced movement need not come into the equation; it can be accomplished by use of the arms and hands alone. It is for this reason that many high-handicap players do have excellent short game skills, but are completely unable to hold their own in long game skills. These golfers are, in fact, turning their short game into something akin to underhanded throwing or lobbing with the one hand – a pure touch-and-feel shot.

The problem facing such golfers is – do they stick to what feels entirely natural to them and works a treat from some hundred yards in to the flag, but leaves them with a very unreliable swing technique for the long game? Or, do they attempt to change both their long and short game towards a more classic style of cross-body balanced swing technique?

My view is that an improved long game technique is much more likely to have an immediate impact on handicap reduction, and one should certainly go for that in the first instance. The short game skills are already established, and will remain. However, if a near classic swing has been achieved in the long game, then I feel that one ought to attempt to keep uniformity throughout the game, and such players would be well advised to take their new found cross-body balanced skills and attempt to adapt a similar technique to their short game.

Putting - Putting is in much the same situation as the short game; it may be a side-dominant or a cross-body balanced technique. Quite obviously, all the better players use cross-body techniques throughout their whole game, be it long game, short game or putting. Their putting style is that of a motionless Vertical Skeletal Unit with the putting stroke confined to the Flail Unit and worked from the two shoulder-blades: in reality, very much like a much shortened "one-piece takeaway" movement. However, even here we are beginning to see more and more variants of the cross-body grip of the hands in professional tournaments these days. These newer-style grips tend to have support from the right hand, but attempt to avoid it having dominant control. This is not so with most amateur side-dominant individuals; most of them perform their putting with their dominant hand in complete control throughout the whole movement; it feels entirely natural to them. The question is, try to change or not?

My answer would be that putting is such a different aspect of the game of golf that one ought to employ the best skills you have available, and, if that means a total and utterly right-side-dominant grip set-up and action, then go ahead and use that technique. Put all your efforts into judging line and length, and use all your skills, whatever technique you use, to get the ball near or into the hole.

I believe that the best putting skills go much beyond mere technique, and it involves an inner gift of judgement of length and line that will reign supreme in this aspect of the game. Some individuals seem to have an extraordinary gift of almost being able to crouch down behind a putt and mentally watch an image of their ball running along their chosen line and being able to judge, with an uncanny precision, whether the ball is on the correct line, or is perhaps going to miss a fraction to one side or the other of the hole. They are then able to reassess and readjust their imaginary line, and watch that ball image go up or down the line again.

Once the line of any putt has been determined, the strength of the putt is in part a mental and visual judgement but it is mostly just a matter of good eye/hand co-ordination, and of what is best termed as a "feel for the greens". If you are a natural, you just tend to let your brain and your hands get on with the job for you; there is no need to think about left, right or both together. Occasionally you may be caught out by not assessing properly the steepness of the green, be it up or downhill. However, that is carelessness, not a faulty feel for the greens. If you possess these sorts of skills, my feeling is that technique is immaterial on the greens.

To sum up. Try for balanced cross-body techniques for the long game and pitching, but my view as regards putting is that any technique that feels natural to you is satisfactory.

A "Regular-Irregular Golf Swing"

During the text I have mentioned the phrase "a regular-irregular swing." What do I mean by this? In my view it is the style of golf swing that will be forced on some thirty per cent of all golfers because of their excessively unbalanced genetic muscular make-up. This so-called 'faulty' swing technique is forced upon them because their inherited muscular component is virtually incapable of being modified to carry out the cross-body balanced movements required of the classic-style golf swing. The only solution left to this large proportion of golfers is to do the best they can with what they have got – a very right-side dominated muscular technique. The currently accepted description of their swings is that they are poor and defective swing techniques and the advice is invariably that they should be altered in an attempt to conform to the so-called correct or classic golf swing. An extremely high proportion of golf lessons and golf literature is devoted to such beliefs.

The truth is that rarely do three or four half-hour lessons make very much difference; perhaps a more stable base may be achieved; perhaps the number of moving parts may be reduced, giving slightly better consistency of shot-making. However, if the player continues to use a right-side-dominant muscular technique to adapt to the suggested changes, the end result is that there will be little or no overall change. There is no disputing the fact that the classic golf swing is the best technique for length and accuracy, because it is both balanced and powerful, and uses every possible body muscle to maximum effect to achieve that balance and power. However, my point is that if you are forced, because of excessive right dominance, to persist with a right side dominant musculature, this will soon be recognised by any Professional. My contention is that, once recognised, it should be appreciated that that golfer is in a different category of golfer, and requires different skills to be taught and explained. My view is that, from that point on, it would be far better to guide that golfer to a recognised and accepted right-side-dominant style of swing. To persist with trying to achieve a so-called 'correct swing' surely cannot be regarded as the best way to help such a player?

With the acquisition of the knowledge we now have about the golf swing, we know how we should guide a player towards a classic style swing; and I believe that there is no harm in every golfer, in the first instance, striving for such a satisfactory end point. However, if it is apparent that it comes at too great a burden in terms of loss of pleasure in one's performance, or simple inability to perform balanced cross-body actions, then I believe there ought to be an alternative, side-dominant, standardised and approved swing technique designed and taught to such golfers. I believe this ought to become accepted as "the correct or perfect golf swing technique for the very right-side-dominant player", and not, as now, thought of as an aberrant swing that must be altered. This would be quite a change in direction from present-day thinking!

I would envisage this swing as being a side-dominant swing technique that was properly documented and taught as a technique that matched with a side-dominant muscular balance. In other words, change the concept away from attempting to match everyone to one mechanical swing technique, and, instead, consider altering the skeletal mechanics and golf swing towards a technique that will match with a right-side-dominant musculature. Aim at a "regular-irregular swing" technique that is fully documented, fully understood and accepted and can be taught with the same authority and belief that it is the correct golf swing technique for excessively right-side-dominant golfers.

Let's explore this concept in a little more detail, as I believe there has to be an arrangement of our skeletal set-up position and skeletal mechanical movements that will match with, and conform to, a right-side-dominant musculature. It is not for me at this juncture to come up with such a swing technique, it merely appears to be the logical conclusion that follows the path I have been pursuing in this book. I would have thought that the development of such a swing technique ought to be well within the scope of the golf's ergodynamic and biomechanical experts.

My thoughts on this, for what it is worth, are that such a technique would have to contend with the concept that a right-side-dominant flail action may well be that of a three-rod flail system performing the bulk of the work, upper arm, lower arm and club shaft. On the other hand, maybe a swing technique such as Lee Trevino's might well fit the bill. His open stance and wrist action, going under and through the ball a short distance, before turning the wrist over, appears to be a very right-side-dominant action.

There was an interesting book written by a club golfer called Mindy Blake. He wrote his book in 1972 and entitled it *The Golf Swing of the Future*. In it, he described what he felt was the golf swing we should all move towards. Unfortunately for him, it did not come to pass, and, I think, for a very good reason. What I feel Mindy Blake actually described in his book was not a swing that could be adopted by the best, but a set-up and swing method that was very much akin to Trevino's technique, and which may well be adaptable to right-side-dominant golfers.

Another thought might perhaps be to adopt a "K" address position, with the ball being addressed and struck from opposite the right foot. I believe the so called "Stack and Tilt Swing" was a posture designed to permit more right-side power coming into the hitting area. It seems to have lost favour, and I assume it ignored the dangers of overstressing one side of the cross-spine action too much, and risked permanent spinal, joint and ligament damage.

The human skeleton is in fact a perfectly designed frame work for a balanced whole body action, and that being so, it seems distinctly odd that our genetic inheritance has come up with two thirds of us possessing unbalanced cross-body muscular control. One would have thought that, as the hunter-gatherers that we once were, we would have genetically bred the human race as extremely athletic cross-body-balanced creatures. But there we are! Two thirds of us are born with lop-sided control of our muscles. If we want to compete with the best, we simply must learn to modify our cross-body muscular balance control – there is no other solution. Being right-side-dominant and following our natural instincts is, as all the evidence shows, a complete waste of time if we really wish for a classic-style golf swing. The solution I have suggested will not be quite the Churchillian "Blood, Toil, Tears and Sweat", but it certainly will be "Determination, Dedication and Devotion to the Cause" – that is, until that all important breakthrough and awakening comes, of what good cross-body balanced action entails. I read, just the other day, in a golf magazine, an article by a world-famous player, in which the player intimated that if one had one's grip, posture and alignment correct, one could hardly go wrong. Oh, if only it were that simple! It isn't, and of the sixty per cent of side dominant golfers who follow my suggestions, with their goal being to achieve a classic swing, my guess is that half of them will succeed, but half will fail, and will be better guided towards an approved right-side-dominant technique – if one can be developed.

At the end of the day, whatever right-side-dominant technique is developed, along with it there may well be the need for some modifications to the design of the golf club itself. Now wouldn't that be a mouth-watering prospect for the multi-billion-pound golf industry! Anyway, I am sure that, if all this could be achieved, it would be an enormous step forward for the hundreds of thousands of club golfers, who, at the moment, are made to feel inadequate, incompetent, and, to a large extent, ignored. I believe that, with a bit of effort by the experts, things could be made so very different.

So there we are! I have explained the basic reasons why we vary so much in our ability to perform a classic golf swing, and given a few suggestions as to how many of us handicap golfers might be able to overcome our problems.

In the Foreword by Harry Bannerman, his short gems of advice contained the essence of all I have been saying – perfect balance and correctly functioning cross-body connections was his theme. Harry is obviously a naturally gifted golfing athlete, most of us are not, and we will have to be shown in rather more detail just how we may achieve these precious gifts if they are not part of our natural inborn instincts.

One last comment, I nearly forgot. The advice that Ben Hogan failed to record for posterity. Quite simple really and I am sure by now most of you will have guessed it. If you want to be a class golfer with a good long game, make absolutely sure you choose your parents wisely! He might well have added — or wait until a certain Neill Kerr writes a short volume on the subject some-time in the future!

Enjoy your golf.